Frenemy

By Garfield Macdonald

Addiction behaviour and drugs

Contents:

Welcome to Frenemy

Hello my name's Garfield. I'm currently 60 years old.

I'm a recovered 'drug' addict.

I started to smoke pot and drink alcohol from the age of about 16. Then I tried speed and acid in my early 20s and then heroin at 28…

I haven't touched heroin or anything else in 12 years.

I smoked it daily for about 12 years. Then on and off for 8 years trying to quit after coming out of rehab at 40.

I haven't drunk alcohol in 30 years, although I never had a problem with alcohol, I think the heroin just put me off it.

I stopped smoking tobacco 10 years ago. I smoked a bit of weed for a while, but haven't smoked anything now for five years…

So I have been abstinent for five years.

I go to the gym daily pretty much. I run 3 km most mornings. I started running five years ago when I stopped smoking. And I joined the gym three years ago.

I believe exercise is all you need. When you exercise you are focusing on your breathing. You are your breath. So when you focus on your breathing, you are truly focusing on yourself.🖤

Healthy body, healthy mind.

I am also working. I've always been a worker – before, during, and obviously after my addiction (I've always had that get off your arse and get it done attitude). I credit my work ethic as a big part of my recovery.

There is a massive difference between doing something for yourSelf, and doing something to make your Self feel better. If you do something for yourSelf, it is coming from you. It requires effort on your part. You're doing it. So you get to keep the reward when the maintained effort of the endured suffering becomes part of you because you get used to it.

So you're bigger, better, smarter, stronger, fitter. You remember the experience, you have an ability now you never had before. You have an awareness and a memory of whatever it is you're learning.

When you do something to make your Self feel better, whatever is making you feel better will not be part of you. Or you are being stimulated by something that isn't part of you, so you'll have to keep doing it because the feeling can't last. And each time you pay attention to the better feeling, you are not paying attention to yourself. Whatever you are paying attention to is called a "false prophet". It requires no effort, so it is an "instant reward". The damage will occur later, but you won't feel it… just like the reward will come later after the endured suffering but you won't feel that either (although you get to keep it). Most people think they know what addiction is about. And they also think they know what an addict is.

So let me ask you a question.

Are you an addict?

I imagine "No!" may be your answer.

Have you ever been an addict?

"No" again!

So if you've never been an addict, it would be fair to say that you don't know what an addict feels like.

If you don't know what an addict feels like…How can you be sure that you're not an addict?

Your answer may be, 'Because I don't use substances or drugs.'

But what if substances or drugs don't actually have anything to do with the damage of addiction?

And what if the damage of addiction doesn't have anything to do with feelings?

What if you never feel like an addict, even when you are? Even if you don't use substance?

So If you don't feel like an addict, despite the fact that you may be one, how will you ever know you are?

What if addiction is psychological?

What if you're never going to feel it, so you're never going to be aware of the damage? Not until it's too late? You may even still be damaging yourself, but have no awareness of it.

All substance does is make you feel better. So naturally, if it makes you feel better, you're not going to feel any damage or addiction.

The drug of choice and the self

So what if addiction is actually caused by feeling better? Or being distracted?

Could this be what is meant by the term "drug of choice"?

Your drug of choice could be whatever you choose to do to make You feel better.

Substance use is just an extreme example of a drug of choice, it's not the only "drug of choice" that we use to feel better.

There's porn, money, fame, power, plastic surgery, food co-dependency, gambling, tattoos, the internet, smartphones, drama, sarcasm social media, etc...

Anything, in fact, that makes YOU feel better.

Have you ever considered that the damage of addiction may not even begin until you feel better?

We can experience psychological damage by anything that makes us feel better, in the same way that someone experiences this psychological damage by using substances. Those who use substances are fortunate enough to have the label of their substance to tell them they have a problem. Yet they still don't believe they have a problem because they don't feel like they do.

The reality is that when you feel better, you lose something. But there are no specific feelings that identify what you're losing, so you don't feel like you're losing anything at all. It doesn't feel like anything is wrong.

It will probably be your lifestyle that lets you know eventually that you have a problem (with substance abuse) but not until it's too late. And that is only because you have a physical dependency on substance.

But what about gambling, social media, porn, etc? There are no physical symptoms there. So there's nothing to tell you that you have a problem.

When you use your drug of choice to feel better, you feel better than You. But there are no specific feelings that identify what You feel like. You're only aware that it feels better because you know what it feels like to be You.

So when you're feeling better, you're avoiding You. The more you feel better, the less you have You as a point of reference and you no longer have anything to compare this better feeling to.

This is when better turns to bitter; when you have lost your balance, lost your ability to be you without a crutch. Then, because you haven't visited that place in so long, it becomes alien. Almost obsolete. It becomes uncomfortable to simply be you without doing something to make your Self feel better. Or to distract you from that place.

This is why you don't know anything is wrong until it's too late. Until you've lost yourSelf entirely. Your drug of choice becomes a little like Stockholm syndrome – the more it devastates you, the more you seek solace from it.

A drug of choice is a false prophet. It'll leave you feeling good, but always wanting more.

The good feeling cannot last because it isn't a part of you.

Which means you'll do it again and again. And each time you do it, you aren't paying attention to your Self, you're paying attention to the way your drug of choice, or your false prophet, makes you feel.

Your false prophet promises you everything whilst simultaneously stealing you from your Self, and you won't know until it's too late and your Self is gone.

Any outside stimuli, anything that isn't part of your Self, anything that doesn't come from you, anything that prevents you from controlling yourself – this is your drug of choice.

Whenever you're being distracted from your current emotional state (ie, your Self) it is by something that isn't part of your emotional state. The distraction always feels better than the Self. But by paying attention to something outside of your Self, you're neglecting it.

You cannot pay attention to both at once. But once again, you'll have no awareness of this because your attention is focused on whatever it is that is distracting you from your Self.

The more you pay attention to the distraction, the less you pay attention to your Self. You become so good at not concentrating that you don't even know you're not concentrating. You've lost all sense of self-awareness.

All the while, you've been gaining new limited experiences under the influence of your drug of choice.

You won't even have that experience without it

And as Whitney Houston said, "I can't run from myself, I got nowhere to hide." This line rings true because as much as you wish to distract yourself using your drug of choice, that uncomfortable and unfamiliar Self you've been running from is always there. It's in the background, annoying you, plaguing you until you become frustrated and anxious.

This is because you've been avoiding your emotional state for so long that you haven't been growing or learning emotionally. This becomes apparent when you lose the ability to communicate properly, but this awareness doesn't come with tools to fix the problem. So what do you do?

You go back to your drug of choice to relieve your Self from the frustration and anxiety. And although it works, for a while, it's compromising you even further and the cycle begins again. Frustration. Anxiety. Drug of choice. This repeats until frustration and anxiety become your permanent state and you're now using these emotions to express yourself. It's as though your drug of choice puts you in an emotionally compromised coma.

😜The human personality as the Self😜

Do you know the difference between yourself and your Ego? In psychology, the human personality is often referred to using a Freudian theory that splits it into three parts: the Id, the Ego, and the Superego.

The Id is the part of us that seeks pleasure and fun and avoids pain and effort. A little like a child, it runs on emotion. The Superego acts as the sensible voice in our heads, like the parent. It's the Superego who keeps us safe and makes most of our decisions. The Ego acts as a mediator between the Id and the Superego, leaving it in a rather conflicted position, constantly battling between the Id (the child) and the superego (the parent).

So one part of our human personality is making the decisions, and the other part is paying the price of them, so in order to alleviate the conflict in the self, we use our drug of choice to feel better.

😱The emotional state😱

I have already clarified that our drug of choice – be it a substance or whatever else we use to feel better – enables us to avoid our current emotional state.

Whatever you use, you're using it in the moment that you feel uncomfortable, frustrated, or anxious.

It functions as a means to distract yourSelf from the present moment, which causes you to lose control of yourself 💜without even realising you've done so💜.

Because the damage of addiction cannot be measured or recognised in feelings, it doesn't exist within the drug of choice itself. The damage of addiction doesn't begin until your Self feels better.

Your drug of choice becomes whatever it is you choose to do to avoid your current emotional state because it acts as a coping mechanism. You might have experienced some sort of trauma or loss and so you avoid that emotional place by using your drug of choice; it's how you cope with it.

⬤ The developing brain ⬤

As we grow as individuals, we mature. We learn to remember things, we learn emotional response and growth, motor function, concentration, discipline, determination, and awareness. We develop confidence and self-esteem and we become secure within ourselves after a series of personal accomplishments and achievements. But we don't feel any of these things any more than we feel dopamine, oxytocin, serotonin or endorphins, because they occur naturally.

We don't physically feel the happy chemicals in our brains, they simply occur.

When we feel good, the part of the brain that controls our behaviour is bypassed, in a sense. And the better we feel, the more this occurs.

We're almost flooded with a dose, but we have no awareness of the fact that we aren't behaving naturally. We aren't growing or learning emotionally.

Our brain functions are still just seeds and as teenagers, they haven't yet developed or matured.

Think back to the emotional coma. Imagine a person suffers a car crash at the age of 20 and is in a coma for 15 years. When they wake at 35, they will still have the emotional level of a 20-year-old. How would that feel?

I would say, just ask a drug addict, or an alcoholic, because that is exactly what addiction does to you.

A drug addict or an alcoholic may be aware by now that this has occurred, but they don't yet have the tools to fix the problem because they're still in their emotionally compromised coma. But when they put down their drug of choice and awaken from it, they'll find out what it feels like.

♥Making excuses

"A big boy done it and ran away!"

We make an excuse for only one of two "reasons". But there's never a reason for making an excuse more than once, because when you make it more than once, it's an excuse.

So we make an excuse either to:

1. Get out of doing something we know we should be doing,

2. Do something we know we shouldn't really be doing.

So the damage of addiction is caused by making excuses (bad behaviour).

It doesn't matter what you make an excuse for, whatever you make an excuse for is called your "drug of choice" or denial (whatever you choose to do to avoid your current emotional state). There are no feelings to identify what an excuse or reason, nor blame or acceptance feel like.

What is the difference between a reason and an excuse?

A reason could be when you had no choice, you had to do the wrong thing despite knowing it was the wrong thing, so you did it once and moved forward making sure, as best you can, that it didn't occur again in future. So you accepted the blame and learned from it. A reason is just once, if you allow it to happen again, it's just an excuse because you should've prevented it from occurring a second time.

An excuse is when you had a choice, you could've done the right thing but you chose to do the wrong thing. You thought you were taking the easy way out because it feels like you're getting away with it. So because it feels like you're getting away with it, it probably won't feel like you're to blame. So if you're not to blame, you haven't done anything wrong, so you haven't got to change your behaviour.

You repeat your behaviour and keep making excuses when it suits you.

This is the damage of addiction.

You are staying in the same place emotionally. You are not learning from your mistakes. You just keep repeating it because you keep excusing it.

And when you keep excusing it, it will feel like it didn't happen).

So when your tolerance builds and your behaviour gets worse, you just keep excusing it because it feels like you haven't done it.

And remember It doesn't matter what you make an excuse for.

Substance use is just one example of something people like to make an excuse for.

Stop making excuses

We have established that it doesn't feel like anything is wrong when you use your drug of choice. But the damage never stops because you're constantly trying to fix it with the wrong methods, with things that damage you further. This is because you're trying to fix something without being truly aware of what it is or where it comes from. And because you're so uncomfortable being with your Self or sitting in your emotional state, you make excuses. You make excuses to avoid your Self at all costs, so you pity yourself and blame external forces. All of this is born from fear and denial – fear of your Self, of the emotional state you're running away from, and denial that the problem is actually you.

Then you're paying attention to anything and everything that is not a part of you and you become judgemental, provocative and critical of everyone and everything else because it's simply another way of focusing your attentions on anything but your Self.

So, you begin with an excuse to take drugs, and then when you've lost your sense of Self entirely, you take drugs all the time. Your tolerance builds up, so do your lies, but it all makes sense in your mind because of the excuses you've created for yourself.

Anything that isn't a part of your Self cannot replace or repair your emotional state. You must look inward and revisit your Self because the only person(thing) who can fix you, is YOU . You must sit and be by yourself with your own thoughts, feelings, and emotions, and move forward with that. You must become reacquainted with your Self. This is how you can finally begin to grow emotionally without the use of outside stimuli or your drug of choice. We only grow and learn as individuals when we are in control of our current emotional state.

Bugsey's "got a brand new squeak".

He's always like this when he's got a new squeak, he wants total possession of it, all of it, now. And you ain't even gettin' a look in.

As you can see by his expression. He won't so much as even look at the camera head-on. Because he's not prepared to give anything away where this squeak is concerned. And being a dog he knows if he so much as acknowledges your existence by looking at you, he's crossing the line – he's giving his power away. Or potentially his squeak, in this instance.

So by not looking at you directly, he's letting you know you're not having anything to do with this squeak. 😊

That's behaviour absolutely brilliantly displayed by a dog, you mustn't cross the line with whatever you're talking about because once that line is crossed, there is no going back.

But we think are smarter than dogs. We don't so much cross the line as push the boundaries. We want our cake and eat it, so we just move the line out the way a little bit LOL.

So what yesterday was not acceptable, today becomes the norm.

Watch that behaviour, peeps. Cos it turns out the dog is smarter than us, cos it knows all about crossing the line.

If you do something once, you'll continue to do it, you'll just have a different (what you think is a) "reason" for doing it, but it's not a a reason, it's an excuse. Because in the end, you just keep doing it until you lose your squeak ...Innit "Bugz.,x

How do I know what I'm talking about? Because I'm an addict. I was an addict before I ever touched drugs. My dad died when I was six years old, and my mum let me get away with murder, so I never learnt to understand my feelings nor my emotional state. But I have no regrets, these are all lessons I've learnt and now, I want to share them.

What I've come to understand is that the problem isn't the drugs, it's addiction. I know this now because I'm on the other side of it. But getting to the other side of it takes time, you have to break it down into achievable parts, like you would a marathon; just one step at a time. And then you have to stick at it. But doing this becomes a little easier when you've learnt to understand yourself and your emotional state - it all begins with an internal understanding.

Focus. Mindfulness. …. Teaches you to pay attention to the moment. The here and now. Be aware in the present moment.

NOW

The past is gone. The future isn't here yet. They are just your memory and your imagination. They are not real. Mindfulness teaches you to pay attention to "now". To concentrate. To focus. But a moment doesn't last so you cannot grasp it. The second you try, it's gone.

So how do you focus on it?

You must focus on something IN the moment. YOU. Pay attention to your breathing, slow it down, focus on it. Focus on that repetitive rhythm and stay there. It teaches you to concentrate and focus on You. You-r. Your breath.

How else are you going to do that if you're not paying attention to yourself? You are the moment. This moment is yours. It is most valuable so spend it wisely.

See? It's gone.

I've written a series of poems that express these lessons I've learnt over the years and they relate to ideas I've touched upon in this introduction. Remember, where using your drug of choice brings you instant reward before it brings you damage or discomfort, getting better works in the opposite way. The hard work brings you discomfort at first, but the reward will follow and you get to keep this one

If I can do it, you can too.

I hope you enjoy my poems, and I hope they teach you a little something you didn't know about yourself.

So, this was the first poem I wrote. I started to become aware of how you feel when taking drugs, but how at the same time you have no awareness of the real damage occurring because you can't feel it.

Eventually, you come to realise you're dragging your heels with regards to your responsibility for yourself emotionally. Everyone who takes drugs will likely identify with this.

We only find out what we are truly capable of as individuals when we push ourselves.

So as my awareness of addiction progressed, so it did through my poems.

Addiction compromises you emotionally so you're never able to express yourself properly. But when I finally put the drugs down, I began to wake from my "emotionally compromised" coma.

Speak the truth and speak it ever.

Cost it what it will.

Because he who hides the wrong he did,

Does the wrong thing still …..forever

♥Praddiction

If you use drugs, I assume you can read

If not, these words I recite

Then tween the lines, if you please

You think you have no drug addiction

Whilst using just once ….may cause an affliction

"I won't get hooked, I know what I'm doin'."

Last famous words. "addictions-a-brewin"

"I don't need it'…. I just wannit."

Is a dangerous assumption

If you use "Cozz you wannit"

In time, you'll just increase your consumption

"I ain't got a problem, I just like gettin' high"

It is the tact   that you take It!
Not how often, or why

They wear their arrogance on their chest like a brooch

Fuckin' lambs to the slaughter

You won't feel its approach

If you practise a desire to use

You being in control is an elaborate ruse

Each time you use, you'll feel high, not afflicted

Well that's exactly when you may becoming addicted

But you won't be aware of its sneaky encroach

You'll be sidetracked with your shiny new brooch

But your shiny new brooch won't sustain you

"I swear !!!!

Do you know why you won't feel it coming??

Because it's already there !!!

You wouldn't walk in front of a bus as it flies down the hill

Well as addiction engulfs you, its affects you won't feel

Every dragon you chase, every joint, pipe or pill

Will leave you in that road at the bottom of the hill

One time you'll be there with little to no fuss

You'll be sat in the road and you won't see the bus

If you Still don't believe these things that I say?
Quick, have another pipe

Bus is on its way 🩶

Most people can identify with this poem, even if they don't use substances, because they will know somebody that has become an alcoholic or a drug addict.

And when they use substances, they feel great and in control, and they feel that they are doing something, or they know something that the alcoholic or addict doesn't. When in reality, the only difference is time. Because the alcoholic and the drug addict have had more time to use more substance.

What the new user doesn't understand is that the alcoholic and the addict at this moment in time, will feel exactly the same on their drug of choice, as the new user does, and crucially that feeling, and awareness will never change.

That's how you end up a junkie or an alcoholic because you never feel like you have a problem, and you always feel like you're in control from the first time you take it. The junkie doesn't feel like an addict any more than you do. Withdrawals are physical caused by a physical substance. There is nothing physical about addiction

This poem carries you into the next one as the awareness progresses.

With this next poem, I wanted to talk more about what it's like, delve a little deeper. This one explains a bit more about what's going on and what the potential damage is about, and also the fact that substances or drugs are just a label.

But this poem still doesn't suggest that drug of choice is anything other than substance.

Always

♥

When you take drugs, you always feel cool

So, you'll never know your eye's off the ball

Instant reward, Perfect Content .....

Your 'get off your arse' has fucked off and went.

Most of the time when you're high, you'll be peaking

You'll also be compromised, emotionally speaking.

You won't 'of course, know this, so you won't feel a fool,

Because you're stoned and happy, so your eye's off the ball.

For your 'drug of choice' you will again yearn

But when stoned and happy, you don't grow or learn

So you take more drugs, which make you feel cool

But now you're stoned and happy for no effort @ all.

Apathy anxiety boredom frustration

All born from your procrastination

So, you take more drugs, which make you feel cool

But now you're stoned and happy but you ain't got fuck all.

Excuse blame pity, we hear

Consequence of your denial and fear

If this all sounds familiar, or at least some of the above

But you still can't quite see it???

Stop taking the drugs.'innit Bugs♥♥♥

The third poem delves even further into the damage to elaborate a little about "drug of choice.

LifeSong

♥

When you take drugs, life's like a song
because it never Ever feels like anything's wrong

But is it because it always feels Great…it's forever appealing

Or Because no Damage or Warning exists the feeling

So, If it does always feel Great and it Never offends
WHY would you ever…stop taking them then?

So, you'll continue to use, but you'll have a compunction

As your tolerance Rises to increase your consumption

Now you're high, most the time
And in a hell of a state,

But you'll never know it
Because it Always feels great

And it's never a reason you can afford

It's just an excuse for your Instant reward

Instant reward is Never a chore

It requires no effort, so you'll always want more

It Always feels great …That is so true

Although when you feel great, you don't pay attention to You

And it will not last, this "wonderful high "

If it's external of you… it don't come from inside

I once met a man who got a tattoo

He ain't got one now, he's got 22

Tattoos or drugs give you a buzz
It is true

But only for a while, because they ain't part of you

Because you feel great, you will persist to take them again because you feel no damage exists

But the damage is occurring
You'll just never know why
While you make an excuse to keep getting high.

And it ain't just substance that's working for you

Remember the geezer that got a tattoo!!

Well now he reckons he's got 89

He's only got 48 really, but that don't rhyme!

You have control and desire in between

Effort, achievement, success, Self esteem

True reward follows effort and it Will Never wane

When you get to keep it ForEver

Because you've now upped your game...

This one is massive because it forces you to look at your Self. And that is exactly what the damage of addiction is about – it is a distraction from Self. It exposes you, you'll know where you are at, and you decide what's going on here whether you like it or not.

As they say, the only lies you have to live with are the ones you tell yourself.

Nuff Rope

What if drugs (substances) have got nothing to do with the damage of addiction?

What if the damage of addiction has nothing to do with feelings?

What if drugs are just a label, the veneer?

What if your "Drug of Choice " is an elephant?

What if your "Drug of Choice " is irrelevant?

What if "all drugs" do, is expose the underlying problem that causes addiction in the first place?

What if that underlying problem is "bad behaviour"?

What if when they said "don't touch drugs"?

They Never Said, 'unless it's "pot" or a few lines at a party… or your partner cheats on you'?

What if "don't touch drugs" means "Any drugs" for "any reason "at "any time" "ever"?

Otherwise you're gonna get damaged and hooked

Why? Well, because you're going to like them, of course …Why else?

What if you feeling the way you do on your "Drug Of Choice"?

"Sound ,… in control…., "this is great"
"I won't get hooked"

…has got nothing to do with you being on your "drug of choice"?

Or the amount of your consumption of it?

Or any other reason excuse or b*ullshit you can come up with, to justify taking it?

Because you will, because you like the way it makes you feel….. "GREAT"

But what if it always feels "Great"?

What if it never don't?

What if nobody ever takes drugs to feel "shit"?

What if nobody becomes addicted to being hit by buses?

What if you never know you're using too much because you pay attention to the excuse you make for doing it, and the reward you're getting out of it?

What if you never feel the   rap

What if junkies and alkis are still waiting to feel the rap .

And what if junkies and alkies never started like that?

You know, ,,,,bang at it, all day, every day.

What if they started like you?

Thinking and feeling that they ain't got a problem?

What if they're still thinking and feeling they aint got a problem?

What if the rap don't exist?

What if you're making excuses for taking drugs?

Most of the people that are taking drugs are smart enough to know they shouldn't

They're just not sure why they shouldn't.
Because they feel good… all the time

But then that's , why ,,,,they make an excuse.

You better be making excuses for taking drugs.

Otherwise, you're too stupid to know you shouldn't even be taking them.

Even the people making excuses are smart enough to know they shouldn't be taking them

That's why they make an excuse

Because they think it counts.

And one day, If the drugs or lifestyle don't kill them first.

They'll realise it never did, does or will do.

What if junkies are making excuses for taking drugs?

What if the only difference between you and a junkie, is time?

What if there is no difference between you and an addict?

What if addictions just….. a woman on a sex ban?

A - Dick-Shun

Keep up Will yer, I'm here all night

What if addictions just denial?

This is where it shifts a gear and goes straight into it. No messing. So now the cat's out the bag, it's all about feeling better. Whatever makes you feel better is called your "drug of choice". But the damage doesn't begin until you feel better and you won't even feel that damage begin. Why? Because you've made yourself feel better, of course.

Here, I begin to open up and explain that the damage has nothing to do with the drug of choice, and everything to do with you.

Rong Path

♥

When you do something to make you feel better

In time it could become your crutch

You only have sex all the time … because you "like it"

But that don't mean you never get fucked…

It ain't what you do, or the "why" that you do it

It is the fact that you do it   too much

What IS an addict

What do you think?

"Someone who takes drugs, someone who drinks"

What "IS " an addict??

Not, what is his buzz?

I asked you what he is

Not what it is that he does!

If he don't feel like an Addict

Although he won't abide with himself

Will he know he's a junkie when he's living in hell

If you never feel like an addict
((Not until it's too late))

No matter how much more substance you take

Then how will you know when you are,,,, "for fuck sake

Feeling Better all the time won't feel like addiction

Never feeling the damage,

Now that's an affliction !!!

If you don't feel like an addict, you may never will

But addiction doesn't care anymore...
...than the damage exists

Not in the way that you feel!

When you feel better, you ain't living in stealth

When you're attracted to something

It distracts you… from yourself 🖤🖤🖤

My previous poems have really been building up to introduce this one. It pretty much explains what addiction and damage is all about. It talks about how you are being damaged, how the damage is a distraction from your Self.

You will become aware after a while you are being damaged. But at the same time, because you can never feel the damage. You can't quite put your finger on how you are being damaged…

You've been aware for a while that there is something missing. You're just not sure what it is

Probably because it's missing. So maybe you can only recognise it when you possess it. Because if you've never had it before, how are you going to know when you're not getting it?

Bearing in mind, the ones that are getting it naturally, can't feel it. This is why all junkies and alkies are like teenagers. Because emotionally, you don't grow and learn as an individual when you start behaving like this. You are not maturing

What does "emotional response and growth" feel like ?

There are no feelings to identify emotional response and growth. So it won't feel like you're losing anything. But you're avoiding your current emotional state.

♥Cajold

Addiction feels like it never begins

Because 'distraction from self' don't come from within

And distraction's an action thats not hard to pursue

When it's caused by an attraction that feels better than you

When you feel better, you're being cajoled Into avoiding your Self

Until you've no Self to control

With no self-control, you'll never be bored

However self-obsessed you've become with your position no more

When you feel better, you're paying a price

But you won't even know it

Because Better always feels nice

But it's just a false prophet, that's only a blast …because it ain't part of you, so the feeling can't last

Feeling better is only appealing because the damage " of course, don't exist in the feeling (or the better).

When you feel better, you never feel bad

But the bigger the better, the more you've been had

Because if you want or need balance in all that you do

What profit's the better, when you sacrifice you?

You may love substance, and although you may not like sweeties, you'll never spit out chocolate because it tastes of diabetes

The damage of substance can be physical, but not just to the letter

The damage of addiction is psychological, and it's caused by whatever makes you feel better

Porn, money, fame, sarcasm, gambling, attention, substance,   tattoos… Only feel better…. for a while, because they ain't part of you

A true 'false prophet' has no remit, and is not part of you, so when you're paying attention to it

You can't be paying attention to you

Addiction, that's It !

This one speaks for itself, but kind of makes even more sense now because of the previous poems

Losin

♥

An excuse feels like a reason

whenever you're deceiving yourSelf into believing
it's you that ain't to blame…

So whenever you're accusin you ain't ownin' it you're choosin' to avoid
your Self ….So you're losin'

Because you're never gonna change

When you shift the blame, you don't own the fault
so you can excuse your Self again ….and again

Until the excuse becomes an action,

Not merely satisfaction, of never accepting the facts
when…. the blame always lies with you

When the action's attribution and it feels like a solution
It's really just an illusion of what you believe is true

♥

A Reason is assurance of ownership…. Endurance,

Accepting blame is Insurance It will not occur again

Addictions like infection from which there's no protection because its merely a
reflection of what you pay attention to

Awareness gives you notice, to always make the most of …your choices.

So, you can focus, on what is best for you

You will forever be betrothed to the consequence of both

A reason for comfort and stagnation or an excuse for strength and growth

With this poem, I've tried to expose the fact that no one escapes. I've used substance as just one example of why people make excuses. The problem is the fact that you make them, not how often or why. Making excuses are distractions which is like keep getting high.

If you make an excuse once, you will do it again when it suits you. So, if you are not careful, you will never learn for yourself. When you make excuses, you stay in the same place emotionally, so you're not learning from your mistake.

SmartAssmug

🩶

I'm not here because I'm the "Yes-Today" man,

But I am here to expose you, because I can

I should start by assuming you ain't no mug

However !

This is a poem of addiction behaviour and drugs

A love sonnet it ain't

So it may seem uncouth

But It's the best way' I know of telling the truth

If you take drugs. it will never end

If you take them

You're gonna like em

So you're gonna take 'em again

But if you "only drink" or "smoke pot"

I'm afraid you can never rejoice

For they are just merely your "Drug of Choice"

Do you know any addicts….. or Alkies

That DON'T excuse their drinking or drugs?

NO. ……They all do, don't they.

And "of course", you have your excuse

"Unless you're a mug "

Now if you're smart, this should play on your mind

The difference between you and a junkie may be a matter of time

The difference between you and an addict may seem obtuse

But you just agreed with me yourself

"All addicts make an excuse."

An excuse feels like a reason whenever it's not

Because an excuse ain't no reason or had you forgot

It's Only a Reason. if you're accepting   the blame

It's just an Excuse if you're gonna do it again

I know you don't feel like an addict or know this is true

The junkie may not feel like an addict
Any more than you do

Your "Drug Of Choice" may give you a thrill

But addiction doesn't care however you feel

You don't think you're an addict because you **always** feel great

But then when they said "don't touch drugs"

They never said "Because you wouldn't…." did they?

All that matters, and this ain't no ruse

You ARE an addict…. if you continue to use

If you still don't believe this cautionary wailing

You won't like it, but you'll BELIEVE it

When your organs start failing

So if you are an addict, what of the

warning you haven't felt yet?

"DON'T TOUCH FUKIN' DRUGS

Is the only warnin' you're gonna get!!!!

This one is just a celebration of what I've learned. (It is always important to distinguish between fact and belief.)

Butterflies

What if birth, is not the beginning

What if death, is not the end

What if they are merely just transition

To a far better place, my friend ..

What if life's not just to wonder why

We physically age and wane

What if we are butterflies upon the wind of Change?

What if the universe is something

You're an integral part of too

Tho Earth goes round the Sun

Your body heals cuts....and fights the flu

What if the universe is conscious

Do you have awareness too?

Uni just means one

But what if it's inverse with you?

Everybody reads, but no one ever looks

What if you don't believe in God

So you don't bother read his book

You don't believe in God
Because you think there is no proof

But what if the Bible really IS the book of Truth?

The book says "God Is Everything"

So anything's allowed

But if that doesn't mean he's in the sky, sitting on a cloud.

What if It means he is anything you want to believe is true

You are also part of Everything

So maybe God Is You!

What if the Bible's just a moral code to keep you pure and true?

To make sure you're paying attention and focusing on you?

What if heaven lies within you?

What if giving keeps you well?

If life is just a balance

What if receiving leads to hell?

What if corruption always lies within what's outside of your shell?

If one's too many

Why is a 1000 not enough?

Be it excuses, buying 'hand bags, tattoos or takin' drugs

Look after your body and it will look after you

It heals cuts, makes babies, cures the flu

"snakes can't talk, the book must be a liar"

But you cannot trust a snake

What if it represented your desire?

Taking drugs or buying handbags will always be a blast

But only for a while because those feelings never last

They are just false prophets on which you can depend

Not just to make you feel good

But to want to feel like that again

Desire has no exception

It offers no surprise

The master of deception

Because it will never be contrived

It only serves to steal your focus

From the way you feel inside..

If you would like to get in touch with me email

Printed in Great Britain
by Amazon